Boats, Boats, Boats

Boats, Boats, Boats

Written by Joanna Ruane

Illustrated by Patti Boyd

My First READER

children's press ®

A Division of Scholastic Inc.
New York Toronto London Auckland Sydney
Mexico City New Delhi Hong Kong
Danbury, Connecticut

Library of Congress Cataloging-in-Publication Data

Ruane, Joanna.
  Boats, boats, boats / written by Joanna Ruane ; illustrated by Patti
Boyd.– 1st American ed.
      p. cm. – (My first reader)
Summary: Rhyming text introduces a variety of boats.
  ISBN 0-516-22922-2 (lib. bdg.)   0-516-24624-0 (pbk.)
[1. Boats and boating–Fiction. 2. Stories in rhyme.] I. Boyd, Patti,
ill. II. Title. III. Series.
  PZ8.3.R83Bo 2003
  [E]–dc21
                                        2003003607

Text © 1990 Nancy Hall, Inc.
Illustrations © 1990 Patti Boyd
Published in 2003 by Children's Press
A Division of Scholastic Inc.
All rights reserved. Published simultaneously in Canada.
Printed in the United States of America.

1 2 3 4 5 6 7 8 9 10 R 12 11 10 09 08 07 06 05 04 03

Note to Parents and Teachers

Once a reader can recognize and identify the 16 words
used to tell this story, he or she will be able to read successfully
the entire book. These 16 words are repeated throughout the story,
so that young readers will be able to easily recognize
the words and understand their meaning.

The 16 words used in this book are:

boats	river
come	sail
green	sea
in	some
me	the
new	too
old	with
red	yellow

Yellow boats, green boats,

red boats, too.

Boats, boats, boats,

11

some old, some new.

Boats in the river,

15

boats in the sea.

Boats, boats, boats,

come sail with me.

Sail in the river.

Sail in the sea.

Boats, boats, boats,

27

come sail with me.

29

ABOUT THE AUTHOR

Joanna Ruane has lived and worked for human rights in Haiti, India, Bolivia, and New York City. *Boats, Boats, Boats* was her first book for children. She currently resides in Brooklyn, New York.

ABOUT THE ILLUSTRATOR

Patti Boyd has been an illustrator for more than thirty years. She lives in Jackson Hole, Wyoming, where she has been actively involved in the business and nonprofit community since 1980. She enjoys hiking, wildlife watching, and her new grandson.